A MOVEMENT OF POETS: THOUGHTS ON POETRY AND FEMINISM

BY JAN CLAUSEN

Long Haul Press
P.O. Box 592
Van Brunt Station
Brooklyn, NY 11215

A version of this essay originally appeared in the *New Women's Times/Feminist Review*.

ISBN 0-9602284-1-1

Produced at The Print Center, Inc., Box 1050, Brooklyn, N.Y., 11202, a non-profit printing facility for literary and arts-related publications. Funded by The New York State Council on the Arts and the National Endowment for the Arts.

*From a world where my poems were as neces-
sary as bread I came into a world where no one
needs poems, neither my poems nor any poems,
where poems are needed like—dessert: if anyone—needs—dessert...*

—Marina Tsvetaeva, 1936

The relationship of poets to the American feminist movement has been, in the decade and more since the inception of the still-unfolding "second wave," remarkable, crucial, and in one sense at least thoroughly astounding. Not that there is by now anything particularly surprising in the assertion that feminism has made possible the recent notable development of women's poetry (what term is, by the way, adequately descriptive of this phenomenon: renaissance? flowering? earthquake? volcanic eruption?); that this tremendous release of poetic energy cannot be understood without reference to the catalytic role of feminism as ideology, political movement, and cultural/material support network. For if we are feminists, so much of what we do has in some sense been made possible by the movement; it seems quite natural that the force which has everywhere in our lives produced transformative bursts of insight, extraordinary and unanticipated displays of creative activism, should have had its impact on our literature as well. More startling—for poets can rarely expect to exert much social influence—is the evident merit of the reverse proposition: that any serious investigation of the development of contemporary feminism must take into account the catalytic role of poets and poetry; that there is some sense in which it can be said that poets have made possible the movement.

It might even be claimed, at the risk of some exaggeration, that poets *are* the movement. Certainly poets are some of feminism's most influential activists, theorists, and spokeswomen; at the same time, poetry has become a favorite means of self-expression, consciousness-raising, and communication among large numbers of women not publicly known as poets. This article represents my effort to grasp the significance of this singular conjunction of a literary form and a political movement—in particular, its implications for the contemporary feminist poet and her work.

It seems to me high time that we attempted such an analysis. The feminist poetry movement has come of age, having been around long enough to have produced a substantial and diverse body of work created by a loosely-knit but vitally interdependent nationwide community of writers. We might even be said to have an historical tradition: the words "feminist poetry" themselves suggest a substantially different phenomenon from the one they might have suggested a decade ago, and it will, I think, be instructive to examine how we got here from there, and to inquire in what direction we may be headed.

However, my *need* to undertake this project really had little to do with such well-reasoned considerations. In fact, I began it in an effort to come to grips with my own situation as a feminist poet; to account for a sense—ill-defined, half-conscious, and ignored for months or perhaps years—of dissatisfaction, blockage, of being somehow hampered in my movements, not only as a writer of my own poems, but as a reader of the poetry of others.

To begin to take this uneasiness seriously has not been a simple matter. I have found it easy enough to blame my inattention to poetry on my involvement with fiction, without really exploring the factors that have made one form more attractive than the other. In part, I have been discouraged from admitting my dissatisfaction by the very success of the feminist poetry movement. The feminist press resounds with the good news of our triumphs: the supportiveness of our networks, the strength of our positive, woman-centered vision, the power of burgeoning consciousness released into speech. What sort of ingrate am I, a published and in many ways privileged feminist poet, to be feeling isolated, at odds with what I perceive as the "mainstream" of feminist poetry? Whatever ails me is probably a private, personal, rather embarrassing affliction best not talked about.

Such, at any rate, has been the counsel of a nagging internal voice I have had to ignore in order to attempt this article, the writing of which has proven extraordinarily difficult. At times, neither my personal perspective nor any generalizations I might attempt have seemed to me likely to interest anyone; at times I've fled the typewriter in tears, feeling quite irrationally that somehow not only the success of this article but the validity of my own identity as a poet, perhaps even as a feminist, was at stake. And yet I have clung to the suspicion that my difficulties and doubts have everything to do with the dilemmas of being a feminist poet, from the basic material level on which I have trouble justifying an investment of time in writing an article on poetry (guaranteed to appeal to a very limited audience and to produce no income whatsoever) to the intellectual and moral level on which I find myself repeatedly hobbled by the fear of saying the wrong thing, of being "politically incorrect" (as we laughingly term it, implying we're far too sophisticated to *believe* in such a concept, much less allow it to determine what we write, or don't). I have clung to the hope of uncovering those tensions or contradictions endemic to a literature embedded in a political movement, a politics largely shaped by literature, which might help to explain my dissatisfactions and uncertainties.

Throughout this writing, one of my major difficulties has been that relationship between the individual "I" and the collective "we" which concerns and to some extent plagues all politically-involved writers. To what degree, I have had to ask myself, is my perspective legitimately representative of that of "feminist poets"? Despite our supposed emphasis on the subjective, I've noticed that the familiar feminist "we" is often used as a substitute for the discredited patriarchal-academic "objectivity" as a means of legitimizing our private perceptions, sometimes even of concealing our vested interests. My awareness of the potential for falsification inherent in this usage has been heightened by those women of color who have vehemently protested the false inclusivity of the white feminist "we"[1]; their experience also suggests the dangers of other exclusions and falsifications. And yet, as I soon enough discovered, to write this article without saying "we" was quite impossible, for it is not only as an individual but very much as a member of a political and literary community that I experience my poet self.

Who, then, is this "we" I have in mind when I speak of "feminist poets"? It comprises poets who not only call themselves feminists, but who confirm that identification through the radicalism of their vision, and frequently of their activism. Many are lesbians of color, non-lesbian women of color, white lesbians; a few are straight white women, though it appears only slightly less difficult for these to cling both to their straightness and to their radicalism than it is for the camel to negotiate the needle's eye. Few are academics; fewer still are academically respectable. Though they share political commitment, they do not share a single feminist ideology: they are socialist feminists, radical feminists, dyke separatists, and all the unnamed shades between and around. Some have important political commitments outside the feminist movement.

I view this motley collection of feminist poets through the lens of who I am: a poet, a lesbian poet, a white self-published lesbian poet slightly over thirty, of middle-class Protestant background, negligible academic credentialing, intense ambition and uncertain "reputation," whose poems have been written and whose literary identity has evolved primarily within the womb/crucible of '70's feminism, a woman-identified radical American poet attempting to face, poetically and otherwise, the vague promises and vivid threats of the second-to-the-last decade of this unprecedented and terrifying century. I am highly conscious that the concerns reflected here are symptomatic of a particular historical moment in the development of feminist poetry—a moment I view, moreover, with the specific geographical bias of a New York City-based feminist and writer. This article, in other words, is but one phase of a process, one facet of a multi-sided conversation. I hope for an answer in the form of assessments from other angles of issues I have raised and others I may not even have considered.

Among the questions I want to explore here are these: What has been the development of feminist poetry over the last decade, and where does it leave us? Why was it poetry and not some other form which came to occupy such a central role within feminism, and what are the implications of that seemingly privileged position? Why has

a movement which has generated such an extraordinary
and compelling body of work produced so little in the way
of critical reflection on that work? In the absence of explicit critical standards, what implicit assumptions and pre-
conceptions about the form and function of feminist poetry,
and the role of the poet, may be inferred? How do these
assumptions affect the poems we write? What is the relationship between the role of poet and that of political
spokeswoman? What are the implications, positive and
negative, of the intellectual and artistic "ghettoization"
which characterizes a functionally separatist literary community? What is the future of an essentially exploratory
literary movement—one dedicated to taboo-breaking, to
investigating the hitherto unspeakable—once the initial
explosive power of self-affirmation in the face of oppression has been tapped? In what ways have we instituted new
taboos to replace the old? What do we, as a movement,
as readers, and as writers, want out of poetry? What can
poetry properly be expected to give us?

The Awakening

The history of participation by poets in American
social and political movements of this century has been
important to the feminist poetry movement. For one
thing it has proven, in the face of the artificial separation
between poetry and politics which the literary establishment
has generally taken such pains to enforce, that there *is* such
a thing as political poetry, and has influenced our ideas of
what that poetry should look like. For another, it has provided examples of women poets, some of them early feminists, to whom we have been able to look for inspiration
and encouragement. The Harlem Renaissance, a chapter of
the Black struggle that was a social as well as cultural movement, was led by poets.[2] Muriel Rukeyser was active in
Left movements from the 1930's on. Gwendolyn Brooks,
Nikki Giovanni, and Sonia Sanchez were closely identified
with the Black Power movement. Denise Levertov, widely
read by feminists in the early '70's, was prominent in oppo-
sition to the Vietnam War. Alice Walker has written ex-

tensively of her work in the Civil Rights movement; Robin Morgan and Marge Piercy of their roots in, and disillusionment with, the New Left.

Yet important as these precedents are in understanding the emergence of the feminist poetry movement, what is perhaps most important and—from a 1980's perspective—most difficult to grasp about the situation of the pre-feminist woman poet is the profound isolation in which she worked. A rereading of Adrienne Rich's 1971 essay "When We Dead Awaken: Writing as Re-Vision" has provided me with a salutary reminder of the consequences of that isolation, one in which a great number of non-feminist women writers are of course still immersed. It is simply impossible for the woman poet working in a male literary tradition to speak in a natural voice of her natural concerns—incessantly aware as she must be, whether or not on a conscious level, of men's judgment of her words, her very being. That woman can be the center of the poetic universe, can be *assumed* as author, subject, and audience of the poem—that is the staggering achievement of the past ten years or so of the feminist poetry movement.

I have my own painful if mercifully abbreviated memories of The Bad Old Days: going through three years of college as a philosophy major, utterly terrified of my school's male literary establishment for whom Gary Snyder was the great poet-guru (how his lines about the girlfriend he once beat up, "drunk, stung with weeks of torment," the two women in the Japanese whorehouse who "dyked each other for a show" still echo in my head; how his career in the merchant marine intimidated me); sitting across from Elana Dykewomon (then Nachman) in "Yeats and Eliot," the one English literature course I took, never dreaming the two of us might have even writing—let alone feminism or lesbianism—in common; soliciting advice on study and reading matter from a male poet with whom I had undergone a humiliating sexual experience; dropping out of school in a desperate, and what then felt quite dangerous, determination to find my own direction; ignoring, at first,

10

the work of Adrienne Rich because it came to me through a suspicious source, my Freudian-oriented shrink who in 1972 handed me a copy of *The Saturday Review* containing some poems from the forthcoming *Diving into the Wreck*.

But why, in my determination to become a "writer," and in my groping, semi-conscious attempts to understand my situation as a woman, did I turn to poetry? And why did poetry come to occupy a similar role in the lives of so many feminists emerging from the social ferment of the 1960's?

Certainly poetry has not always been the genre women have found most accessible. In nineteenth century England it was the novel, a relatively new, popular, and less prestigious form, which was seen as appropriate to women.[3] Poetry was upheld as the highest and purest of the literary arts, most difficult because of its rigid formal requirements—the province, hence, of aristocrats by birth, education, and/or "genius" (read: white men of the middle and upper classes). But American women struggling into feminist consciousness were the beneficiaries of a populist literary tradition, stretching back into the nineteenth century, which had established the possibility of a poetry close to everyday speech.[4] Fiction—The Novel—had come to be perceived as the major literary form; poetry now appeared less intimidating, at least to most would-be *writers*. (Ironically, the "poetry anxiety" traditionally instilled in high school English classes seems to persist in many feminist *readers*, resulting in the twin axioms familiar to feminist poets that "women don't read poetry" and "poetry doesn't sell.")

Important material considerations favor poetry as a "woman's form." Poetry seems the easiest thing to write under conditions of interruption or limited time—though, interestingly, Virginia Woolf argued the opposite in *A Room of One's Own*: "Less concentration is required," she says of fiction.[5] Poetry is cheaper to self-publish than fiction; more easily fitted into such public contexts as the anthology, the newspaper, or the open reading; and probably offers the beginning writer a surer bet for acceptance in periodicals.

I know I began with poetry because it seemed the easiest thing to write—which is to say, at least remotely possible. It was blessedly short, for one thing, and therefore meant less of an investment of time and energy than a story, which would obviously have to go on for several pages. But perhaps even more important was the fact that I didn't think of poetry as "made up" in the same sense as fiction. A poem, it seemed to me, would be an authentic and therefore unchallengeable record of my feelings, perceptions, and experiences —whereas if I "faked it," fictionalized, I felt I somehow became more vulnerable to external, probably male, standards. I now see these issues very differently, recognizing the "fictional" possibilities of poetry and the way that an author's personal experience is central to all prose fiction, whether or not literally autobiographical. But the point is that I had to learn to speak in poetry: it seemed, initially, the only way for me to be certain of owning my own voice.

I think that for many feminists, as for me, poetry represented the clearest opportunity for the direct statement of women's experience; it was the literary counterpart of the C-R groups' attempt at breaking down the distinction between the personal and the political. In the beginning, we had an enormous appetite for *the evidence,* for anything that could provide testimony concerning the conditions of women's lives. Every woman's story was to be told and listened to, and poetry was one way of accomplishing this. Almost anything a woman wrote seemed important, simply because a woman had written it. (But that statement is both true and false; many of us, white and well-educated, were comfortably naive in our assumptions about the universality of our exploration, arrogant in our attempt to construct, from a very limited perspective, what we thought of as the total picture.)

The connection between poetry and feminism was intense and immediate. Fran Winant said of her activity during this period:

> I wrote many of my poems specifically for the open
> poetry readings that were considered important at the
> start of the women's movement. The knowledge that
> there was a place for my work to go, and an all-women's
> audience to listen to it, immediately made me able to
> write about my personal experiences and feelings as I
> never could before.[6]

(Note that she implies open readings were no longer popular by 1975, when this statement appeared.) The early, influential commercial press anthology on women's liberation *Sisterhood Is Powerful*, edited by poet Robin Morgan, included as a matter of course a section entitled "Poetry as Protest."

Initial feminist interest in poetry took two forms: an intensive reading and gathering together of previously published poetry by women from Sappho to Sylvia Plath, and an outpouring of new poetry, much of it shared through open readings, via the pages of small and "underground" periodicals, or in the form of hastily assembled books and pamphlets issued by the first feminist publishing efforts. In either case, "I am a woman" was the core revelation sought or expressed. Anger, as Adrienne Rich noted, was omnipresent, for the focus was frequently on the circumstances of women's oppression within patriarchy.[7]

The selection of commercially available contemporary poetry embraced on political grounds during this phase might strike us today as startlingly eclectic. Often it was enough that the poet be a woman; she need not necessarily be a feminist, and she was highly unlikely to be a lesbian, or at least not openly so. Possibilities included work by June Jordan (*Some Changes*, E.P. Dutton, 1971); Denise Levertov; Marge Piercy (then published by a university press); Muriel Rukeyser; Sylvia Plath and Anne Sexton, those enormously influential poets of female anger and victimization; early Erica Jong; middle Diane Wakoski; Nikki Giovanni's extremely male-identified *Black Feeling, Black Talk, Black Judgement* (William Morrow and Company, 1970); and Diane diPrima's equally male-identified

Revolutionary Letters (City Lights Books, 1971). I remember seeing selections from the last volume, in particular, admiringly reprinted in feminist newspapers.

It is interesting to note how many of these poets (not, of course, all) have lapsed from feminist fashion, or met with feminist wrath. A friend of mine reports, for instance, that by the mid-'70's she felt considerable chagrin at having to admit she was writing a dissertation on the once-idolized, but now "non-feminist," Plath. As late as 1974 I jumped at the opportunity to take a workshop with Jong, a distinction I had become reluctant even to mention only a year or two later. And it is a sobering experience to note the virulent homophobia and anti-Semitism in Giovanni's early-'70's work (as it is, for that matter, to read early "underground" heroine Rita Mae Brown's musings on the joys of owning a Rolls Royce in a recent issue of *Savvy*[8]).

Though it lacked commercial distribution advantages, the grassroots, "underground" poetry scene enjoyed those of ad hoc immediacy: a poet could publish new work in a pamphlet or newspaper days or weeks after writing it. Such poetry satisfied a demand for poems explicitly feminist in their perspective, flourishing in the gap between the explosion of feminist consciousness and the commercial publication of feminist poetry anthologies and individual volumes.

Much "underground" publishing was then, as it is today, in fact self-publishing. Many of the poets involved were lesbians, and a number wrote out of their experience as working-class and/or Black women, as well.[9] The Women's Press Collective published Judy Grahn's *Edward the Dyke and Other Poems* in 1971, and Pat Parker's *Child of Myself*—originally issued by Shameless Hussy Press—in 1972. Alta, founder of Shameless Hussy, also published her own work and early work by Susan Griffin. Rita Mae Brown's *The Hand That Cradles the Rock* was issued by a university press in 1971 (and reissued by Diana Press is 1974). Fran Winant self-published her *Looking at Women* (Violet Press, 1971) and subsequently compiled *We Are All Lesbians* (Violet Press, 1973), the first lesbian poetry anthology.   Audre Lorde published four small press poetry volumes before her first commercially published book appeared in 1976. In her capacity as poetry editor of *Amazon Quarterly*, the influential lesbian magazine founded in 1972, she became one of a very few women of color to have exercised editorial control over even a portion of a nationally distributed feminist periodical in the past decade.

A transition to increased commercial publication of explicitly feminist poetry began in 1972, the year in which Robin Morgan published *Monster*. Adrienne Rich's *Diving into the Wreck* appeared the following year. These books by white women, one by a new poet already known for her feminist activism, the other by a well-established poet for whom it marked a turning to explicitly feminist concerns, enjoyed the advantages of commercial promotion and distribution.   The two volumes were in a position to exert enormous influence on a large feminist audience, shaping its idea of "feminist poetry," and of the poet as activist and theorist.   Also in 1973, Alice Walker's second book of poems, *Revolutionary Petunias*, was published commercially, and Broadside, a small Black press, issued Audre Lorde's *From a Land Where Other People Live*. The Lorde, Walker, and Rich volumes were nominated for the National Book Award in the following year. Rich accepted the award, given for *Diving into the Wreck*, on behalf of all three poets, reading a collective statement which rejected the divisiveness and tokenizing implicit in the awards process.

The years 1973 and 1974 also saw the commercial publication of three widely distributed, influential poetry anthologies edited from a white, mainly heterosexual feminist perspective: *Rising Tides* and *No More Masks* (1973) and *The World Split Open* (1974). *We Become New* followed in 1975. Along with the National Book Award nominations, these publications apparently constituted the high water mark of establishment and commercial press interest in feminist poetry; other such mass market anthologies have not been forthcoming. They made a significant contribution to the widespread availability of "women's poetry"—

predominantly that of white heterosexual women. The volumes, however, do include significant selections by a few Black poets, and Louise Bernikow's introduction to *The World Split Open*, which acknowledges the historical correlation between women's poetry and woman-loving, was of particular significance in the development of lesbian poetry. Poets of color who are not Black are strikingly absent from these volumes, as they have been from my discussion so far: at this point white feminists, to the extent that we transcended white solipsism at all, still thought overwhelmingly in terms of a Black/white dichotomy.

Mid to Late Decade: The Cultural Separatist Alternative

Two major and interconnected developments of the mid-'70's helped to modify the omnivorous early emphasis on "women's poetry." The first of these was the increasing prominence of openly lesbian poets, a phenomenon largely reflective of the emergence of lesbian-feminism as an influential tendency within the women's movement. The second was the growth of the lesbian-led feminist press movement with its encouragement of a functional cultural separatism. As a result of these trends, what appear in retrospect to have been two parallel feminist poetry movements—a largely lesbian underground of insurgent small press poets, and a largely heterosexual "mainstream" of commercially published poets—fused into what might be characterized as a lesbian-feminist poetry movement with non-lesbian adherents.[10] This was a movement focused less on examining the conditions of women's subjection than on moving out, as Adrienne Rich had forecast in 1971, toward "the boundaries of patriarchy."[11]

During the mid-'70's, for instance, "establishment"-certified Adrienne Rich and Marilyn Hacker came out publicly as lesbians; small press-published Audre Lorde and Susan Griffin began to publish commercially; and Olga Broumas received the Yale Younger Poets award for her explicitly lesbian first collection. Despite the visibility resulting from commercial publication of lesbian poetry, however, the feminist press movement remained the mainstay of lesbian literature, and such lesbian poets as Ellen Marie Bissert, Karen Brodine, Alison Colbert, Willyce Kim, Irena Klepfisz, Jackie Lapidus, Joan Larkin, Susan Sherman, Lorraine Sutton, and I published small press first volumes.

Several of these lesbian writers are Third World (Willyce Kim, Asian-American, and Lorraine Sutton, Puerto Rican). Important work by other women of color was also introduced by a few feminist small presses at this time: Shameless Hussy Press published first volumes by Black poet Ntozake Shange and Japanese-American poet Mitsuye Yamada in 1975, for instance. Sunbury Magazine and Press presented the poetry of a number of women of color, including that of Sutton in 1975, and volumes by Jodi Braxton and Rikki Lights (who are Black) in 1977; Kelsey Street Press published Chinese-American Nellie Wong's first collection in the same year.

By the mid-'70's, Diana Press and Daughters, Inc. had emerged as relatively powerful, well-organized lesbian-controlled publishing efforts. Out & Out Books issued its first titles in 1975, among them *Amazon Poetry: An Anthology*, the largest collection of lesbian poetry then available, and the most comprehensive through the end of the decade. *Amazon Quarterly* ceased publication in that year, but Audre Lorde subsequently became poetry editor of *Chrysalis*, begun in 1976—as was the more explicitly lesbian-focused *Sinister Wisdom*. *Azalea*, a magazine by and for Third World lesbians, and *Conditions*, a magazine of women's writing with an emphasis on writing by lesbians, began publication in 1977. Throughout the mid-'70's, most feminist presses and periodicals published substantial amounts of poetry; the major exceptions, Diana Press and Daughters, Inc., were nevertheless extremely important to lesbian poets because of their role in the development of a specifically lesbian-feminist literary culture and community.

Interesting evidence of this emerging culture is to be found in *Margins* 23 (1975) and *Sinister Wisdom* 2 (1976), both edited by Beth Hodges, both with a focus on lesbian writing and publishing. The latter included my article "The

Politics of Publishing and the Lesbian Community," which discussed the results of a questionnaire survey I had conducted among lesbian-feminist writers. Responses suggested that a number of lesbian writers had at that point become rather defensive about their publishing choices. The article —and the defensiveness—were in part occasioned by a vociferous campaign conducted by June Arnold and Parke Bowman of Daughters and Coletta Reid of Diana, who maintained that it was the duty of feminist writers to publish their work with feminist presses.

Now that the dust of that old debate has settled, it is easier to see that, couched in radical-sounding rhetoric, what Arnold, Bowman, and Reid offered that was attractive to feminist writers was a middle ground between the uneven production, poor distribution, and nonexistent royalties of the early feminist press efforts, and the exploitation, insensitivity, and undependability of the male-controlled commercial presses. Feminist writers, they promised, could have it both ways: they could sustain their radicalism *and* reap professional rewards, be both politically correct *and* paid. Lesbian-feminist literature need not subsist on patriarchal crumbs. It should emerge proudly from its "underground," peripheral status and, declaring itself "major," expect to succeed on its own terms—through the creation of feminist institutions which (if enough feminists supported them) could hope to compete with "the boys."

The lack of realism inherent in this ambitious program is perhaps suggested by the fact that both Daughters and Diana ceased publishing activities shortly after formulating it. And certainly not all lesbian-feminist writers (let alone heterosexual feminists!) were comfortable with the implications of narrowness and rigid definition lurking in the air of the time and manifested also, for instance, in the phenomenon of doctrinaire lesbian separatism. However, the impulse towards an autonomous feminist culture has continued into the present, as has the trend towards increased professionalization of publishing efforts and writing careers, at least by contrast with the poetry "underground" of the early '70's.

If "I am a woman" had been the central proposition focusing the poetic explorations of early-'70's feminists, then "I am a lesbian" was by mid-decade the resounding theme. Certainly I recall feeling it was the message the poetry audiences I encountered at that time overwhelmingly wanted and expected to hear. I suspect that this expectation influenced perception of (and perhaps self-presentation by) poets like Irena Klepfisz, Audre Lorde, and Susan Sherman, for whom lesbianism was, though important, not necessarily their primary subject. For other poets—the Olga Broumas of *Beginning with O*, the Susan Griffin of the newer poems appearing in *Like the Iris of an Eye*, and the Adrienne Rich of "From an Old House in America" and *The Dream of a Common Language*—the declaration "I am a lesbian," interpreted not merely in a sexual sense but as self-affirmation, proclamation of independence from patriarchy, and assertion of the primacy of emotional bonding among women, was indeed at the heart of their work.

"The Assumptions in Which We Are Drenched"

"Until we can understand the assumptions in which we are drenched we cannot know ourselves,"[12] Adrienne Rich wrote in 1971. She was thinking then of the need for feminists to examine the assumptions of patriarchal literature, but it seems to me that the observation is equally applicable to the anti-patriarchal poetry which feminists have since striven to create. So far as I am able to identify them, I want to investigate the nature and implications of the assumptions which have influenced the creation of feminist poetry. I will do so before going on to discuss recent developments, partly because these assumptions seem to me largely the product of the two phases of feminist poetry I have so far discussed, partly because I think that an understanding of them helps to illuminate the shifts and transformations of the current period.

My task here is made more difficult by the absence of much in the way of written theory or analysis of feminist poetry as a general phenomenon. To the extent that we have produced it at all, our "criticism" has generally been limited to reviewing, or at the most to articles focusing on the work of a single poet; with a few exceptions, several of which are discussed below, feminists have not written about what feminist poetry is or ought to be. Symptomatic of this situation is, for example, the fact that although poetry has certainly been at least as prominent a form of literary endeavor among lesbians as fiction, almost all theoretical discussion contained in the *Margins* and *Sinister Wisdom* issues on lesbian literature and publishing focuses on the latter form; even an article comprehensively entitled "Lesbian Literature: Random Thoughts" by Cathy Cruikshank ignores poetry. Similarly, the discussion of contemporary lesbian writing in Lillian Faderman's recent *Surpassing the Love of Men* is concerned almost exclusively with fiction.

What does this dearth of criticism say about the feminist view of poetry? Do we believe, as some of us were once taught about sex, that poetry is supposed to "just happen," that talking about it will ruin the romance? Or do feminists share the contemporary American prejudice that fiction is the major form, the one worthy of serious attention? Whatever the case may be, I do not believe that the absence of articulated criticism signals a corresponding absence of assumptions about how a feminist poem should look (or sound) and what it ought to do. Instead, I think that we must often look to the poems themselves, or to comments poets and readers make in extra-poetic contexts, to identify implicit assumptions. Precisely because they are unstated, such assumptions may at times function more tyrannically than would explicit "standards," particularly for the younger or less experienced feminist poet.

A poet friend told me this: at a point when her style had changed in the direction of a longer, looser poetic line, someone remarked of her earlier work that perhaps she'd been trying too hard to write "feminist poetry." When I asked what that meant, she explained that initially she'd been heavily influenced by the work of Pat Parker, Judy

Grahn, and Robin Morgan, with the result that she set out
to write poems which she saw as communicating very directly with audiences of women in the way those poets' work
has done. She also expected a concentration on "women's
issues" (e.g. rape) and use of traditional "women's forms"
(e.g. a folk song form) to offer the ideal poetic embodiment
of her feminism. Eventually she discovered she could more
satisfactorily explore her feminist concerns in a style she
felt was influenced by Tennyson and other male poets she'd
read in earlier years.

Though the feminist poets of the early '70's must frequently have felt almost intoxicated by their sense of feminist poetry as a clean slate, an open field, the truth was that
feminist poetry was not being created in a vacuum. It was
from the start "anti-patriarchal," almost bound to be de-
fined, negatively, in contrast to what was perceived as the
male poetry tradition.[13] Much, I think, has been either
self-imposed or self-excused on the grounds that it is as unlike what "the boys" do as possible. Consider, for instance,
one woman's reply to my objection to a review in which she
had, among other things, badly misquoted my poetry: that
she "wasn't like the *New York Times*" and "tried to be as
creative as possible with her reviewing."

But almost anything can be shown to be unlike what
some male poet or critic has done. Just what are these assumptions with which a beginning poet may have to grapple
—and against which, I suspect, a more experienced poet may
continue to measure her work, even while heeding the im-
perative of her "own voice"? I am about to sketch what
amounts to a caricature of feminist poetic practice; happily,
it does not constitute a standard to which we universally
adhere—otherwise our poetry would be flat, stuffy, and bor-
ing, which, at its best, it certainly is not. Nor are these assumptions unchanging: the "ideal" feminist poem of 1971
might have looked somewhat different from its 1981 counterpart.

Feminist poetry is useful. Usefulness seems to be one
of the most universal expectations of feminist poetry, as it

has been, historically, of "political art" in general. (For example, "Art is a weapon" was a characteristic Communist slogan of the 1930's and later.) Here is a passage from Karen Brodine's "Politics of Women Writing," one of the very few discussions of the practice of feminist poetry to appear over the past decade:

> I have yet to know the use of a poem the way I know the use of a hammer. Yet I feel a poem is surely a tool. My friend who works as a gardener says that only after months of learning to work with tools, did she realize they are not foreign objects, but simple extensions of the hand. So our writing should not be some awkward object or product, but an extension of our feeling/dream/belief....
>
> Part of the use of art is its ability to express the ideas of the movement. The strongest writing today expresses the contradictions of this society.[14]

Judy Grahn makes a strikingly similar statement in "Murdering the King's English," the introduction to *True to Life Adventure Stories*; her remarks seem applicable to poetry as well as prose:

> Art, in my terms, is like a basket, and a basket is useful....
>
> Women's art, feminist writing, has a definition which I have used in this anthology: it must be useful to women, must work in our interest. Must not work to divide us further, must not lie about us to each other, must not give false information which would fall apart when people try to make use of it.[15]

Note the slipperiness of these "definitions." A tool implies the existence of some specific, consciously-held objective in the service of which it is employed, an analogy inconsistent with the amorphous "extension of our feeling/dream/belief" toward which Brodine's passage shifts, while Grahn avoids specifying *how* she gauges art's usefulness, detailing instead what art must *not* do. (How, I wonder, can we be sure that the telling of a hard truth will not "work to divide us further"? How can we be certain in advance that the information we give will not "fall apart when people try to make use of it"?)

22

I see prescriptions of this sort as dangerous because they seem to call for a conscious control which I believe poets do not, or should not, always have. In our efforts to "express the ideas of the movement," or "work in [women's] interests," we are too likely to go over old, safe territory, rather than undertaking explorations whose usefulness is not, and may never be, readily apparent.

I am troubled by the defensiveness about art which the insistence on poetry as tool or utensil seems to reveal—as though feminists will be unwilling to keep art around unless it can be shown to pay its own way. Defensiveness is similarly reflected in that leftist euphemism, sometimes heard in feminist circles, "cultural worker"—the implication being that art has to be justified by the pretence that its creation resembles standing on an assembly line eight hours a day.

A study of earlier political-literary movements—the various Communist ones, for instance—reveals striking parallels to these utilitarian analogies, suggesting the commonality of certain issues and concerns to artists working within seemingly divergent political contexts.[16] But the mesh of poetry and politics within feminism appears at first glance to go far beyond the historically familiar scenario according to which writers have served as appendages to political groups, flimsy cultural "superstructure" tacked onto the solid political "base." And yet some feminist poets, in their sincere desire to be politically effective, have adopted a view of art which betrays a fundamental suspicion of its workings, requiring that it justify its existence on the basis of what it can be demonstrated to *do*.

A seemingly very different expression of feminist desire for a useful poetry is seen in the stress certain poets place on the transformation of language as a key to the transformation of reality itself. Olga Broumas writes:

> I am a woman committed to
> a politics
> of transliteration, the methodology

of a mind
stunned at the suddenly
possible shifts of meaning—for which
like amnesiacs

in a ward on fire, we must
find words
or burn.[17]

"It was an old theme even for me:/Language cannot do everything," Adrienne Rich remarks, yet goes on to admit that "what in fact I keep choosing/are these words...."[18] The "dream of a common language" is for her far more than metaphor for connection—as the "politics of transliteration" would appear to be for Broumas. "Language is as real, as tangible in our lives as streets, pipelines, telephone switchboards, microwaves, radioactivity, cloning laboratories, nuclear power stations,"[19] Rich reminds us elsewhere. Judith McDaniel, appearing at the 1977 Modern Language Association on a panel entitled "The Transformation of Silence into Language and Action," said:

> ...I can't talk about language and action in separate modes. Language for me is action. To speak words that have been unspoken, to imagine that which is unimaginable, is to create the place in which change (action) occurs. I do believe our acts are limited—ultimately—only by what we fail or succeed in conceptualizing. To imagine a changed universe will not cause it come into being, that is a more complex affair; but to fail to imagine it, the consequences of that are clear.
>
> If feminism is the final cause—and I believe it is—then language is the first necessity.[20]

These poets, far from being apologetic about the possibilities of their chosen medium, make rather grandiose claims for it. Despite their disclaimers ("language cannot do everything"; "to imagine a changed universe will not cause it to come into being"), it is hard to come away from a reading of the works in which the passages I have quoted appear without feeling that for these writers the politics of language actually take precedence over other politics.

Perhaps such an emphasis is quite natural for a poet; after all, it is because of our intense involvement with the power of language that we *are* poets. But feminist poets tend also to take on roles as theoreticians and political spokeswomen. And the blurring of distinctions between literary prominence and political leadership has meant that sometimes feminist theory and practice have been skewed in the direction of too much stress on the transformation of language, too little emphasis on the other sorts of transformations which a political movement that hopes to succeed in the material world must undertake.

Or perhaps the causal relationship goes the other way; perhaps it is in part precisely because of what a Marxist would call an "idealist" bent in our movement, a weakness for mind-over-matter approaches, that poets have emerged as leaders. This would help to account for the popularity of such feminist thinkers as Mary Daly, who has focused almost exclusively on language as a vehicle for feminist transformation.[21]

It seems to me that this inflated expectation of language may ultimately lead to the same predicament invited by those who would have us see poetry as tool or utensil: the placing of an intolerable burden on poetry. Apparently feminist poets have in common with other political writers a tendency to require of our poems feats which elude us in real life. We expect our poems to be "positive," to offer, if not a comprehensive solution, at least a clear direction, an optimistic program which in fact may amount to not much more than a ringing declamation of "the people united will never be defeated" against the evidence.[22]

I have struggled with my own expectations along these lines. Particularly in trying to conclude long poems that I felt represented "major statements," I have racked my brains for a suitably positive note, feeling that my failure to find it would somehow constitute a *political failure*. And how could I read my poem from the plaform to the audience at the benefit, rally, or "cultural event" if I could not match Judy Grahn's promise, "death, ho death/you

shall be poor"; if I could not echo June Jordan's threat, "...
from now on my resistance/my simple and daily and nightly
self-determination/may very well cost you your life!"; or af-
firm, with Susan Sherman, that "Your enemies are endless
Amerika/...By our life   we will finally/destroy you/Even as
you try to level us/with your death"?[2][3]   In fact, the three
poems which end with these lines are strong and moving,
but their impact seems to rest more on our *desire* to believe
their closing assertions than on the intrinsic credibility these
assertions possess based on what we know of the world or
the evidence the poems themselves present. A little of this
technique goes a very long way; the danger it poses is of the
slide into rhetoric, the rote chanting of slogans we are un-
able to make real, the temptation to dish up to the audience
what it wants or has learned to expect in the way of ex-
 hortation and uplift.

In her essay "Poems Are Not Luxuries," Audre Lorde
suggests a view of poetry as neither mundane tool nor in-
strument of quasi-magical transformation, but as closely
akin to dream in its functioning in our lives. (I find interesting, by the way, the defensive implications of her title—
evidently she perceives a danger that poems *will* be seen as
luxuries.) For her, poetry is "illumination," "the quality
of light by which we scrutinize our lives":

> When we view living, in the european mode,
> only as a problem to be solved, we rely solely upon
> our ideas to make us free, for these were what the
> white fathers told us were precious. But as we be-
> come more in touch with our own ancient, black,
> non-European view of living as a situation to be ex-
> perienced and interacted with, we learn more and
> more to cherish our feelings, to respect those hidden
> sources of our power from where true knowledge
> and therefore lasting action comes. At this point in
> time, I believe that women carry within ourselves
> the possibility for fusion of these approaches as a
> keystone for survival, and we come closest to this
> combination in our poetry. I speak here of poetry
> as the revelation or distillation of experience, not
> the sterile word play that, too often, the white fa-
> thers distorted the word poetry to mean—in order

to cover their desperate wish for imagination without insight.[24]

I find Lorde's questioning of the view of life "only as a problem to be solved" particularly suggestive. I am swayed by her belief in the possibilities of a poetry which can be of use, not in a narrowly utilitarian sense nor one which undervalues the place of action in the world, but as "the revelation or distillation of experience."

Yet I would like to request feminists to entertain at least briefly the seemingly perverse and heretical notion that it may be poetry's stubborn quality of rockbottom, intrinsic *uselessness* which—despite all the useful things it is sometimes observed to do, from eliciting that "CLICK" of feminist recognition that *Ms. Magazine* is so keen on, to drawing crowds at the latest fundraiser—constitutes the guarantee of its integrity, and hence of its ultimate value to us. No matter how we seek to disguise the unpleasant fact, a poet remains a person whose life is essentially unjustified and unjustifiable: her most basic task, her "calling" (of course she will have many other occupations) is simply to *be*, to experience, and to metabolize that experience through the process we call poetry. This view of the poet is reflected in the following engagingly defiant passage by the Russian poet Osip Mandelstam, whose bad attitude was his ticket to the Stalinist labor camp where he died:

> No matter how hard I work, whether I carry a horse slung across my shoulders, whether I turn millstones, I shall never become a worker. My work, regardless of the form, is considered mischief, lawlessness, mere accident. But I like it that way, and I agree to my calling. I'll even sign my name with both hands.[25]

The very success of feminist poetry, accustoming poets to expect relatively enthusiastic audiences and a relative degree of prestige or acclaim, requires us, I believe, to remind ourselves that a poet's work may or may not connect directly and immediately with hearers; may or may not produce some tangible material result or some far-reaching transformation in consciousness—in the here-and-now, or ever. These factors are often beyond a poet's control, and they should not be taken as a measure of feminist commitment or political responsibility.

If it's results you're after, hire an organizer.

Feminist poetry is accessible. This assumption surely has its origins at least in part in feminist poetry's anti-patriarchal premises: men's poetry is inaccessible, therefore ours will be accessible. (In fact, there is a tradition of male political poetry which also values accessibility; Pablo Neruda changed his style drastically in an effort to make his work less obscure, for example.) However, the concept of accessibility is seldom examined critically, and in the absence of such evaluation, one unfortunate connotation seems to be *easiness*, instant comprehensibility. Adrienne Parks, in her 1975 essay "The Lesbian Feminist as Writer as Lesbian Feminist," asserts:

> Lf audiences tend to understand lf writings, song, art, etc. without any difficulty. Their expectations of what is being offered coincide both with what is actually offered and with what their own experience tells them is "true to" the lf experience.[26]

In fact, the poetry which is most clearly *not* inaccessible is that which draws a predictable laugh at the reading, elicits the response, "Hey, I can relate to that"—the poetry which makes a direct, unambiguous statement. All of us have enjoyed such poetry, but is it really what we want exclusively to cultivate? What about poetry's ability to "mean" several or many or even contradictory things all at once, its trick of defying translation and synopsis? What about its musical qualities, and the *listening* with the whole being—not just the rational part of the brain—that this calls for? Is "accessibility" merely a matter of employing short, commonly-used words? Of renouncing traditional forms? Does it imply the necessity of making use of concepts, feelings, subject-matter which will threaten no one, because they are comfortably familiar to all? Stereotypes and cliches are, by this standard, eminently accessible.

I think the feminist obsession with accessibility reflects, in part, the process of intimidation that begins early in school, where we learn to be afraid of feeling stupid when we are not sure what literature, and particularly poetry, means. What we are almost never told then is that even people with lifetimes of practice often have a hard time deciding "what a poem means." What if, instead of trying to resolve things by demanding that every poem state its business as efficiently as though coughing up name, rank, and serial number, we affirmed each reader's right to approach poetry in her own way?

We do need to examine seriously the class functions of language and literary forms, and to reject the tyranny of "standard English" which has functioned so effectively to hush and to exclude. Judy Grahn's "Murdering the King's English" is an important, and courageously forthright, step in this direction. So is June Jordan's "White English/Black English: The Politics of Translation."[27] I do not, however, believe that those of us who are most comfortable with standard English should renounce our use of it—or that the solution to problems of class and literature is likely to be found in what Michelle Cliff, discussing a Third World woman's criticism of parts of *Claiming an Identity They Taught Me to Despise* as written in "inaccessible language," characterizes as literary downward mobility:

> The one thing that saved me all these years coming out
> as a lesbian, being a woman of color, was the ability to
> read and to write....

> ...I think we, Black women specifically, have an enor-
> mous literary tradition and have knowledge of it and
> there is this pretense that we should be downwardly mo-
> bile to reach everybody which I don't think is necessary.
> I find it very much like economic downward mobility
> which I don't particularly care for either. Once you
> have the privilege, if you want to reject it that's fine,
> but if you've worked hard for your education it doesn't
> make much sense.[28]

Unfortunately, feminist discussions of privilege and language are seldom so direct and public. Instead the subject is surrounded by an intimidating silence that has its parallels in other art fields. I am thinking, for instance, of a composer who discovered her work was being scorned as unfeminist because her influences were classical western ones. Not that she was told so directly—her friends let her know what was being said behind her back.

Feminist poetry is "about" specific subject-matter: oppression, woman-identification, identity. It avoids both traditional forms and distancing techniques such as persona and third-person narration. It is a statement of personal experience or feeling, with the poet a first-person presence in the poem. These assumptions have their origins in the initial impulse of many feminist poets to reclaim their own experience, and to express that experience in ways they could be sure had not been imposed from without. For feminists deeply immersed in the consciousness-raising process, it was the authenticity of fact, the truth of each woman's direct testimony—not that of the imagination, or of observed experience—which was central to poetry.[29]

Certainly the past ten years have produced an impressive body of work which meets these criteria. Certainly, too, some feminist poets have consistently written other sorts of poetry—I think, for instance, of Irena Klepfisz' frequent use of persona, Marilyn Hacker's fondness for rhymed forms—but to the extent that they have done so, they tend to seem somewhat anomalous. (My own experience suggests that this sort of "deviation" frequently makes it extremely difficult to decide what to read to feminist audiences.) Again, the danger is that of adopting a knee-jerk anti-patriarchal stance, and thereby limiting the possibilities of feminist poetry.

Sometimes narrow expectations of "the feminist poem" can constitute a particularly outrageous violation of the poet's being and vision, as happened several years ago following a reading (by someone other than the poet) of Audre Lorde's "Power," her reaction to the murder of a young Black boy by a white policeman: a white woman remarked that Lorde "was focusing too much on racism and not enough on sexism." Aside from the fact that racism *is* a feminist issue, Lorde's poem is an unmistakably female and, I think, deeply feminist statement about racism; it is as inconceivable to me that a Black man could have written that

30

poem as it is that a white woman could have done so.

Women are affected by absolutely everything that goes on in the world, and it is the right and necessity of the feminist poet to explore whatever occupies the center of her field of vision. Even that poetry which is most directly based in the poet's real life is something more than raw experience; art always selects and shapes. Recognition of these facts can perhaps free us to consider possibilities of subject matter and form which have so far not been typical of feminist poetry.

Feminist poetry is a collective product or process; the individual ego plays a minimal role in its creation. This assumption (or perhaps "aspiration" would be more accurate?) evokes the tension between the "I" and the "we" which I discussed at the beginning of this article as chronic for political writers, who have sometimes been asked to submerge the "I" altogether. An extreme example of a piously correct position on this issue was exhibited by a poet with whom I read at a recent political event. She had, she announced, requested to be introduced by name only, without mention of any publications or affiliations, because she regarded her work as a simple and direct expression of the voice of The People. I'm not sure whether this particular leftist poet calls herself a feminist, but she certainly got an enthusiastic response from a largely feminist audience.

In her essay "Thinking About My Poetry," June Jordan gives an interesting and perhaps useful account of her own changing approach to this issue, based on her activism in the Black community:

> Toward the close of the sixties, I...decided that I wanted to aim for the achievement of a collective voice, that I wanted to speak as a community to a community, that to do otherwise was not easily defensible, nor useful, and would be, in any case, at variance with clarified political values I held as my own, by then....

> But a few years into the seventies, and I reconsidered again; aspiration toward a collective voice seemed to me conceitful, at least....it did seem to me...that if I could truthfully attend to my own perpetual birth, if I could trace the provocations for my own voice and then trace

its reverberations through love, Alaska, whatever, that then I could hope to count upon myself to be serving a positive and collective function, without pretending to be more than the one Black woman poet I am, as a matter of fact.[30]

More prevalent among feminists than insistence on a collective voice is our emphasis on the collective process of feminist poetry, its emergence from a network of mutual influence and support without which our work would, for most of us, be inconceivable. Melanie Kaye, in her essay "On Being a Lesbian-Feminist Artist," enthusiastically expresses this spirit of interdependence:

> I have passed around my copies of Wittig's *Les Guèril-léres*, Toni Morrison's *Sula*, Arnold's *Sister Gin*, until pages fall out. My sister in New York, I in Oregon, discover on the phone that we have each been profoundly shaken by Adrienne Rich's piece on lying. I gather with sister poets to celebrate Gertrude Stein's birthday by reading her work on the radio. This is a circulatory system that shows me we are one body: the network is literally vital.

> ....

> One of our tasks as feminist writers is to preserve and expand the identity we have labored to record and create.

> As women, we need this identity to survive. As writers, these connections enlarge what we can say. They enable us to speak less personally, without lying or distance but because we are seeing and feeling less personally; that is, less separately....I pass on to women not only what I have to say, but what has been said to me. *In every sense, we do not work alone.*

> ....

> We are seeing in this decade a gathering of demands on artists to tell the truth(s) about female experience. I write for an audience who requires responsible work, an audience who shares to an extent unprecedented in twentieth century poetry a sense of common concerns. We grow together or not at all: this we know.[31]

I am in sympathy with much of this, but am disturbed by what is missing, the other side of the picture that is typically slighted in discussions of this sort. What happens when we sense that what we are experiencing is *not* echoed in the work of other women, when we feel isolated despite the existence of the community, when we find ourselves at odds with or bored by much of what feminists write? These discordant sensations are all the more difficult to cope with when we are busy telling each other that artistic alienation and isolation are diseases confined to privileged male poets.

Poems like Adrienne Rich's "Transcendental Etude" have told us what our creativity ought to be:

> Such a composition has nothing to do with eternity,
> the striving for greatness, brilliance—
> only with the musing of a mind
> one with her body, experienced fingers quietly pushing
> dark against bright, silk against roughness,
> pulling the tenets of a life together
> with no mere will to mastery....[32]

But what happens when we fall short of this ideal, when we detect in ourselves motives akin to the ambition and competitiveness of the virtuoso, that male creator with whom this poem suggests we should have nothing in common? Generally, our response is denial: ambition and competition are simply not considered topics suitable for mention in public, certainly not in print—which means that we forego the chance to investigate them calmly and honestly. I am afraid that this failure may condemn us to repeat the lesson suggested by Rich's grim vision of Marie Curie, who

> ...died   a famous woman   denying
> her wounds
> denying
> her wounds   came   from the same source as her power[33]

What we have going for us as women, I believe, are not "better" emotions and motives than men, but the chance, if we will take it, to be truthful with ourselves and each other about them.

Where feminist poetry is concerned, criticism is politically suspect—or irrelevant. In a mid-'70's interview first published in *Big Mama Rag*, Pat Parker remarked:

> All standards seem to exist to obscure meaning. I just
> want to *say* what I mean. Poetry has been controlled by
> men for so long. They've set the standards, the criteria
> for what's a good poem. It's all a bunch of shit, aca-
> demic wanderings.[34]

Her statement reveals a good deal about the origins of an anti-critical attitude which has been quite common among feminist writers in general, perhaps particularly those whose identities—race, class, or uncompromising public lesbian-ism—have rendered them especially vulnerable to damaging establishment prescriptions for the writing of "literature."[35] Too, criticism has understandably not been a priority for wo-men who often enough have had their hands full just getting the organizing done and the poems written. And, as I re-marked earlier, for some mysterious reason poetry seems to receive less of what meager critical attention *is* accorded to feminist work than does fiction.

Our criticism is further held back by the familiar con-fusion as to just what is an authentically feminist criticism—which translates roughly as: how honest can a critic be about negative reactions and still be considered feminist? Some re-viewers who have tested this out have generated public con-troversies; most prefer to play it safe with positive or non-evaluative reviews. Marge Piercy, in a letter published in *Sinister Wisdom*, sums up her own perspective on this issue in re-freshingly trenchant fashion; her evident anger says some-thing significant, I think, about the extent and consequences of public pressure on feminists not to be critical:

> If we cannot tell the truth as we see it, if we cannot be
> honest in women's publications for our own audiences,
> when do we tell the truth? Never? Then let's cash it all
> in now. If reviewing means patting on the head and on
> the fanny in mindless approbation whether we think
> what is being done is worth the price of admission or
> not, then it's patronizing mush. Traditional feminine
> behavior. "Oh, darling, you look fantastic in that dress."
> Then afterward, "Where did she get it? That's the sort
> of thing your maid gives you when she wears it out."

Class example intentional, because we're discussing,
after all, ladylike behavior. Be nice in public. Say
something nice no matter what you think. After all,
you can say in private what you like later on.[36]

As a poet, I know that I want and need to think analytically about other poets' work, and that I benefit from external perspectives on my own. I am grateful for the serious considerations of feminist poetry which occasionally appear in print; for the periodicals which make space for reviews and criticism. Too often, however, I find myself enraged by yet another narrowly academic article (typically, one which either focuses, in a manner utterly compatible with the pursuit of tenure, on some dead white straight poet, or discusses Adrienne Rich's work without recognizing she's a lesbian)—or by some three-paragraph review which turns out to be sloppily disrespectful even on the minimal level of "plot summary." Unless more feminists who care for poetry adopt careful criticism as a conscious, publicly espoused priority, I do not see how this state of affairs can be expected to change.

The world of feminist literature is sufficient unto itself; the feminist poet need look no further for inspiration, audience, or support. "Admit it," a writer friend said to me one evening (we were, it so happens, discussing fiction, but it might as well have been poetry), "you want *them* to have to take you seriously." She didn't have to tell me who *them* meant—I who every week read the *New York Times Book Review* from cover to cover, groaning and cursing throughout. Her remark was not an accusation. We were enjoying one of those small private gatherings in which heresies may safely be aired, and she was simply acknowledging our common—and highly "incorrect"—ambition.

I sometimes have the sense that I live my life as a writer with my nose pressed against the wide, shiny plate glass window of the "mainstream" culture. The world seems full of straight, large-circulation, slick periodicals which wouldn't think of reviewing my work and bookstores which will never order it, because small press stuff doesn't plug into the nexus of commercial publication which proclaims an author worthy of serious notice, and because even the cover reveals that I'm focused on the "narrow concerns" (to use the code phrase I've been encountering lately) of the lesbian-feminist.

It doesn't help much to remind myself that all "minority" writers encounter this business about narrowness (while we are flooded with books exploring the broad concerns of white straight upper middle class professionals), or that the literary establishment is riddled with corruption, homophobia, myopia, sexism, racism, and just plain stupidity. It doesn't help because, unlike Adrienne Parks, I don't experience an automatic fit between my "lesbian-feminist art" and the "lesbian-feminist audience." In fact, I'm not so sure that a randomly picked lesbian-feminist would be any more likely to have a positive response to my poetry than a randomly picked anybody else female, except perhaps that she'd be less likely to be frightened off by the dyke label. And if there are a couple of men out there somewhere who are interested in what I have to say, I'm not too proud to have them for readers, either. But the existence of this non-lesbian audience remains largely hypothetical; as a self-published lesbian-feminist poet, there are too many places my books simply cannot go.

I sometimes find myself thinking of life in the feminist literary community—even in bustling New York—as "life in the provinces." This is my private, rueful phrase for a feminist literary existence which, both for reasons of our choosing and ones not of our choosing, tends to be extremely isolated from other literary communities, the work they produce, and the resources and opportunities they offer at least some writers some of the time. (This is not just a matter of our distance from the literary establishment, but from other dissident literary groupings: Black literature which is not explicitly feminist, for example, or the less reactionary facets of the white-male-controlled small press movement.) The problem involves not only audience, but also the ingrown nature of our publishing networks, the underdevelopment of criticism, and our narrow—and narrowing—assumptions about what a feminist poet ought to read, what influences she should permit herself.

What is the meaning of my secret relief at learning that a poet I like and respect has dared to be influenced by Tennyson? What about my astonishment at June Jordan's celebration of Whitman's influence on American literature (a *Black feminist* poet recommending a *white male nineteenth century* one?)—followed by pleasure at the thought that I'd been given "permission" to reread *Leaves of Grass?* What does it mean to label *any* writer incorrect or off limits (as June Jordan does Emily Dickinson in that same essay)?[37] Why is this such a necessary exercise for us, the division of the world into the permitted and the forbidden? I find it significant that, following an extended period of boredom with poetry, it was my reading of work by Bertolt Brecht and Osip Mandelstam which rekindled my enthusiasm, and eventually prompted the writing of this article—leading me, in turn, to an appreciative rereading of much feminist poetry.

To say that I believe the assumptions outlined above have sometimes unhealthily constrained feminist poets is by no means to belittle our immense achievements. The fact that many of the issues discussed here have preoccupied writers connected with other political movements suggests that they are basic matters which could neither have been avoided nor easily resolved. But I have thought it important to suggest that our poetry has hardly been the medium totally lacking in standards and prescribed forms which we have sometimes proclaimed it to be. I also think it important to make explicit "the assumptions in which we are drenched," rather than adding to their power over us by adhering to positions of public correctness, airing our doubts and deviations, if at all, only in private. Finally, I think that this discussion suggests one possible reason for the perceptible flagging of feminist interest (specifically *white* feminist interest) in poetry in the period following the lesbian poetry renaissance of the mid-'70's: what had begun as an anti-traditional movement had to a certain extent developed its own dogmas, conventions, cautions, cliches, taboos.

Seventies into Eighties

> Do I dare speak of the boredom setting in among the white sector of the feminist movement? What was once a cutting edge, growing dull in the too easy solution to our problems of hunger of soul and stomach. The lesbian separatist utopia? No thank you, sisters. I can't prepare myself a revolutionary packet that makes no sense when I leave the white suburbs of Watertown, Massachusetts and take the T-line to Black Roxbury.
>
> —*Cherríe Moraga, Introduction to* This Bridge Called My Back

The most significant development for feminist poetry in the past few years has been, so far as I can see, the emergence into public voice of a large group of feminist poets of color—Native American, Asian-American, or Latina as well as Black. Many of them are lesbians; most have managed, with considerable difficulty, to get their work published by the white feminist or male-controlled small presses, or have resorted to self-publication. (Ntozake Shange and Alexis DeVeaux are the commercially published exceptions I am aware of.) These poets join with the prominent Black feminist poets so frequently isolated and tokenized by white feminists, thereby creating a movement-within-a-movement of great power and vitality.

For example, in addition to feminist poets of color mentioned in my earlier discussion of mid-'70's feminist publishing, recent years have seen the appearance of volumes by Indian/Native American poets Paula Gunn Allen (*The Blind Lion*, Thorp Springs Press, 1975 and *Coyote's Daylight Trip*, La Confluencia, 1978), Joy Harjo (*The Last Song*, Puerto del Sol Press, 1975 and *What Moon Drove Me to This*, I. Reed Books, 1979), and Linda Hogan (*Calling Myself Home*, Greenfield Review Press, 1978); Chinese-American poet Fay Chiang (*In the City of Contradictions*, Sunbury Press, 1979); Japanese-American poet Barbara Noda (*Strawberries*, Shameless Hussy Press, 1980); Black poets Joan Gibbs (*Between a Rock and a Hard Place*, February 3rd Press, 1979) and Michelle Cliff (*Claiming an Identity They Taught Me to Despise*, Persephone Press, 1980); and Chicana poet Alma Villanueva (*Mother, May I?*, Motheroot Publications, 1978). Meanwhile, Chicana poets Gloria Anzaldúa and Cherríe Moraga have edited *This Bridge Called My Back: Writings by Radical Women of Color* (Persephone Press, 1981), an important collection including poetry and a number of essays expressing "an uncompromised definition of feminism by women of color." Some other significant sources for poetry by feminists of color include the multi-ethnic *Ordinary Women* (1978); *Conditions: Five,* The Black Women's Issue (guest-edited by Lorraine Bethel and Barbara Smith, 1979); and *Lesbian Poetry: An Anthology* (compiled by white editors Elly Bulkin and Joan Larkin, Persephone Press, 1981). The ongoing publication of *Azalea:* A Magazine by and for Third World Lesbians, and the recent founding of Kitchen Table/ Women of Color Press, offer hope for the development of this poetry independent of the control of white editors and publishers.

In certain ways the emergence of this body of work recalls the emergence of early white feminist poetry: these poets are exploring oppressions and drawing on reserves of experience and tradition which have hitherto seldom entered literature. Theirs is the energy of anger released when growing consciousness hits the flashpoint of precise articulation (and this includes much anger at white feminist racism); the discovery of anciently-rooted strengths; the radiant energy of new forms of female connection. In this sense, the poetry of women of color belongs specifically to them: it is a literature white feminists can learn from, enjoy, support—but from the sidelines. In another sense, however, I think that much of this work points a direction for the entire feminist poetry movement—toward a complexity of vision, away from "too easy solutions." This is a journey that requires of us a courageous scrutiny of what is most frightening and destructive in ourselves as well as in the world outside us.

Feminists of color, and particularly lesbians, have rarely found in women's communities or in feminist ideology the refuge from painful complexity which has been available there, albeit at great cost, to some white women. Black feminist poets have been saying this loud and clear all along: Audre Lorde in much of her poetry and prose; June Jordan in her "Declaration of an Independence I Would Just as Soon Not Have"[38]; Pat Parker in this description of her rebellion against labelling of her poetry: "...I'm advertised as lesbian poems, fuck poems, kill the whites poems. Sometimes I feel I'm not angry enough to be billed this way....If I'm advertised as a black poet, I'll read dyke poems."[39] Their insistence on complexity now resonates with the work of such poets as Cherríe Moraga and Gloria Anzaldúa (see their essays, and Moraga's poetry and introductory remarks, in *This Bridge Called My Back*); Jamaican-born Michelle Cliff, for whom "claiming an identity" has meant investigating and coming to terms with the intersection of Blackness and whiteness in her own heritage; Native American Chrystos, whose extraordinary pieces in *This Bridge Called My Back* range from an expression of rage at white feminist racism ("I Don't Understand Those Who Have Turned Away From Me") to self-questioning regarding her own complicity in the destruction of the planet ("No Rock Scorns Me as Whore").

Similar issues of identity and responsibility are alive for some recently published white feminist poets as well. Melanie Kaye (*We Speak in Code*, Motheroot Publications, 1980) writes out of her Jewish working-class background, lesbian reality and activist consciousness. Minnie Bruce Pratt's *The Sound of One Fork* (Night Heron Press, 1981) expresses both love for her southern rural environment and her efforts to understand and reverse the patterns of racism in her life.

I referred earlier to the trend towards increased professionalization of feminist poetry which began to be apparent in the mid-'70's. This has continued, with a move from small press to commercial publication (only for a few well-known poets, however); increasing sophistication about production and distribution methods on the part of small press and self-publishers; and the proliferation of feminist writers' conferences and privately-run poetry workshops. In 1978 Melanie Kaye offered the following perspective on this trend:

> What I see now in most places is a regrouping of hierarchy, of *women* writers this time: poetry as performance rather than dialogue. Important women, women with book or books, read longer, get paid more, are flown in to places like Portland, and to some extent get treated as stars. I say this without accusation. I myself have profited from this formation....And I think this evolution occurred for reasons. More women began writing, open poetry readings got longer and more chaotic, our unwillingness to apply alien standards of criticism made us chary of applying any standards at all (beyond the occasional not very useful one of "how right-on is this?"); and we got bored with what sometimes seemed repetitive.
>
> The danger is that the space which allowed me and many of us to become writers has been enclosed, filled, and made inaccessible to new women, except through an old-girls network of workshops and who-one-knows. We all have stories, they should be told.[40]

In addition to the reasons Kaye lists, certainly economic pressures on poets have encouraged this process. Early in the movement, the writing, reading, and publishing of feminist poetry were often taken for granted as volunteer efforts—as they generally continue to be for poets whose work is little known. Few of us imagined that writing could ever become a source of income; in fact, the necessity for time-consuming, energy-draining jobs was one reason to write poetry rather than novels or books of feminist theory. But volunteerism becomes increasingly exhausting as the years go by, and poets' efforts to parlay writing into an income source inevitably lead to at least some degree of professionalization. Poetry readings become job opportunities of a sort; the teaching of workshops may provide a supplemental income making it possible to squeeze by on unemployment, an adjunct lectureship, or a halftime clerical job rather than a full-time one.

Ironically, though material circumstances may originally dictate the writing of feminist poetry, they may end by discouraging it. For once income from writing is seen as a real possibility, it becomes evident that any significant sum is far more likely to come from prose. Besides, readers are so clear in their preference for prose! I have had some first-hand experience of these pressures myself recently: earning about a thousand dollars from my fiction collection over the past year certainly hasn't supported me, but it *has* begun to make fiction seem more like legitimate work, and poems (or this article) like self-indulgence. Meanwhile, after years of peddling poetry to a largely reluctant public, having fiction received graciously and often with thanks feels like a dangerously addictive pleasure.

Whatever the reasons, though most of the feminist poets of the early- to mid-'70's have continued to publish new poetry, a number have become heavily involved with other forms as well. (It is interesting to note that the reverse process—writers known for their prose turning to poetry—almost never occurs.) Adrienne Rich and Susan Griffin have published influential works of feminist theory; Judy Grahn has edited several volumes of "True to Life Adventure Stories" and is at work on a book of prose; Audre Lorde's most recent book publication is *The Cancer Journals* (Spinsters, Ink, 1980) and her "biomythography" is forthcoming from Persephone Press; Marge Piercy and Alice Walker, both of whom have been ambidextrous in poetry and fiction over the past decade, are now probably far more widely known as fiction writers than as poets.

Contemporary feminist poetry is marked by a broadening of focus which characterizes the feminist movement in general; we are perhaps somewhat less intense and concentrated than we were five years ago. For poets this may mean, for instance, more room for sonnets and sestinas as well as for resolutely anti-formal poetry; for publishing options all the way from separatist volumes put out for lesbians only (such as Elana Dykewomon's *fragments from lesbos*, Diaspora Distribution, 1981) to commercial press collections.

I find these developments generally encouraging, though it isn't always clear to me to what extent they indicate a true pluralism, rather than a drifting apart, a slackening of once-taut bonds which permits mere uneasy, even grudging, co-existence. Certainly I am exhilarated by the extraordinary range of themes and styles to be encountered in *Lesbian Poetry: An Anthology* (Persephone Press), which contains the work of sixty-four living American lesbian poets, and whose 1981 publication to an enthusiastic reception is in itself encouraging evidence of the continuing vitality of feminist poetry.

But the phase of initial exploration, of poems written, often enough, in the creative heat of the feminist "conversion experience," and necessarily in symbiosis with a dynamic, expanding political movement—that phase seems definitely over. *I am a woman; I am a lesbian*: for so many white feminists, especially, these bald, obvious sentences stand for tremendous revelations which, during the early and mid-'70's, formed the core of our lives and poetry in a simpler way than they could (we may now see) have been expected to do indefinitely. Yet for many who lived through it, feminist poetry's "heroic age" will, I think, be hard to let go of, move away from both in expectation and in practice. What, we may uneasily inquire, can we do for an encore?

The Possibilities of Poetry

In considering the future of feminist poetry, we cannot very well avoid the dismal material realities and political conditions which will inevitably affect its creation. Grants to the arts, especially those with any sort of progressive political content, are seriously jeopardized. (While I was working on this article, an attempt was made in Congress to excise the *entire* Literature Program from the budget of the National Endowment for the Arts.) Women's studies becomes an increasingly narrow, often reactionary area of academic concentration. Librarians are being given every reason to exercise caution in their acquisition of feminist—and certainly lesbian—materials. Any book with serious feminist content is now more likely than ever to be shunned by commercial publishers. Marginal enterprises like feminist newspapers, magazines, presses, and bookstores—upon which the development of feminist poetry has been so heavily dependent—are ill-situated to withstand the combination of severe economic and political pressures increasingly likely to be exerted against them. The issues, of course, extend far beyond the realm of the arts. As the organizers of the October, 1981 Women in Print conference stated with chilling brevity: "The rationale for the conference is survival. The survival of the women's movement, as of any revolutionary movement, depends directly on that of our communications network."

It may be argued that feminist poetry, never having been heavily subsidized by government or other institutions, is in a relatively good position to withstand these onslaughts. After all, even those of us who've forgotten how to crank a mimeograph machine can easily refresh our memories. But self-publishing, too, becomes increasingly difficult in hard times, and we're likely to be surprised at what a difference even small grants and occasional gigs made, once they are gone.

Still, these factors seem to me no more important than the negative effects the ominous political climate is likely to have on our own view of ourselves as feminist—as female—poets. The fragility of the public context which has enabled us to place women at the center of the poetic universe—to do so *as a matter of course*—cannot be overemphasized. The erosion of that context in a period of reaction will inevitably mark our work. And it will even more certainly and stringently constrict the efforts of the next generation of women poets (and affect how our own work is remembered, or forgotten)—if, indeed, human society is so fortunate as to survive into the next century, and at a level of organization which permits ongoing literary endeavor.

We have no choice about these extremely unpleasant facts, apart from whatever we are able to do in the political realm to stem them. But we do have a choice of responses.

An obvious temptation seems to be the retreat into a new feminist literary orthodoxy, a withdrawal further into an insular, functionally separatist literary community. As a defensive measure, such a response seems to me understandable, but also a serious mistake, likely to result in claustrophobia, boredom, and both political and literary sterility.

One thing we can and should do instead, I believe, is to start taking poetry more seriously. For as a movement, we are far too used to the assumption that poetry and poets will be *there* when we want them, no matter how long they have been ignored, taken for granted, misused. After all, isn't poetry a form of prophecy, and aren't prophets known for their talent for flourishing in inhospitable deserts and other bleak surroundings?

Maybe. But maybe not indefinitely.

What do I mean by "misuse"? By "taking poetry seriously"?

I think, first of all, that the attempt to control poetry, to subordinate it to extra-poetic ends, constitutes misuse. And, as I suggested earlier, I think we have often made this attempt—not even necessarily conscious that we were doing so. I am not, of course, advocating "art for art's sake": poetic values are ultimately life-values, deeply political values. But those values must emerge from the poetry, not be imposed on it. And it is particularly difficult for the feminist writer dependent upon a small, relatively homogeneous community for her support and audience to ignore narrow political expectations about poetry. Poetry will always be found to have uses, and we will want to evaluate the relationship between our consciously espoused *ideas* and our literature. But the most difficult thing to remember from within the context of a political movement, with its emphasis on ideology and on results, is the need to be open to the unconscious, the unforeseen, the unplanned.

I believe we might benefit from what I think of as an increased "separation of powers"—those of the poet and those of the political leader. The blurring of the roles of poet and political spokeswoman has given feminist poetry a

range of influence it might otherwise not have enjoyed, and
has to some extent infused feminist organizing with poetic
values, but it has also sometimes led to an overemphasis on
words, language, and the ideas these embody—and to the
placing of an impossible burden upon poetry. Feminism des-
perately needs actions as well as words. And while I firmly
believe that poets should be activists, that is not to say that
they are necessarily best suited to provide practical, tactical
leadership.

I think we further misuse poetry when we present it in
such a way as to make of it a spectacle, an entertainment ex-
travaganza, or a branch of political speechifying. Again, this
is a matter of degree, of emphasis. There is a place for the
marathon poetry reading with its circus atmosphere, the ob-
ligatory "cultural event" at the political rally. But when
these become the main or the only settings in which feminist
poetry gets heard, there is a serious problem, an inevitable
distortion of what gets read and what the audience is able to
absorb. Such contexts are bound to encourage in poets the
impulse to court easy laughter and easy applause; they are
simply not conducive to the serious listening which poetry
requires and deserves. Poets themselves are going to have to
insist on better reading/listening conditions, if these are to
materialize.

In other ways, too, we need to make more of an effort
to provide access to feminist poetry. The understandable re-
luctance of most feminist small presses to publish it (a great
deal of the feminist small press poetry in circulation is *self*-
published) on the grounds that it "doesn't sell," and the re-
luctance of feminist bookstores to stock it (except for a few
well-known, commercially-published titles) on the same
grounds, or because "there's so much feminist poetry
around," may in the long run have serious consequences—
like the channelling of poets into the writing of prose.[41]

Ironically, I suspect that poetry as a genre has lost
prestige within the women's movement for the same reason
that fiction lacked it in nineteenth century patriarchal Eng-
land—because it is perceived as something almost anyone can

do. That is the hidden meaning of a code phrase like "there's so much feminist poetry," and it points to the hypocrisy of the general feminist rejection of critical standards: rather than apply them, we have sometimes simply stopped paying attention to poetry at all. This seems to suggest that the development of feminist criticism may be more vital to the health of feminist poetry than we have realized.

But suppose we make an effort to do all these things, to provide a context which takes feminist poetry seriously. What about the essential task, the poetry itself?

While preparing to write this article, I read the following in Adrienne Rich's 1975 essay "Vesuvius at Home: The Power of Emily Dickinson":

> It seems likely that the nineteenth-century woman poet, especially, felt the medium of poetry as dangerous, in ways that the woman novelist did not feel the medium of fiction to be....Poetry is too much rooted in the unconscious; it presses too close against the barriers of repression; and the nineteenth-century woman had much to repress.[42]

Later I discovered these lines, written in the early 1950's by self-exiled Polish poet Czeslaw Milosz:

> The objective conditions necessary to the realization of a work of art are, as we know, a highly complex phenomenon, involving one's public, the possibility of contact with it, the general atmosphere, and above all freedom from involuntary subjective control. "I can't write as I would like to," a young Polish poet admitted to me..."I get halfway through a phrase, and already I submit it to Marxist criticism. I imagine what X or Y will say about it, and I change the ending."[43]

I have since been haunted by the implications of these passages for contemporary feminist poets and poetry. "What do *we* have to repress?" my notes inquire. I expect that our own corsetings and evasions will appear (*if*, again, the human community survives) quite as sadly obvious to poets of a hundred years hence as those of nineteenth century women poets or twentieth century poets bound by the strictures of doctrinaire Marxism appear to us.

One vast area of uneasiness which suggests the workings of repression has been that of questions surrounding whatever privilege we may ourselves possess, whatever processes of oppression and destruction we participate in. In my own work I notice, and am increasingly disturbed by, the enormous difficulty I experience, not only in *mentioning* certain topics (particularly, for me, race and class oppression) but in approaching them honestly and directly, avoiding the sterility of carefully manicured "correctness." Some recent work (for instance, poetry by Minnie Bruce Pratt and much of the material in *This Bridge Called My Back*) demonstrates encouraging evidence of attempts to breach this "barrier of repression."

Though issues of female anger (particularly anger at men) and female sexuality may have become somewhat less tabooed for us recently, the problem of our own power often remains, I think, as thornily central as it was for Emily Dickinson—and is therefore another significant area of repression, one closely related to questions of privilege. Given our history as women and that of the world at large, there is no way for us to avoid the negative connotations the concept of power inevitably suggests—though many feminists have tried to solve the problem by that act of repression which involves positing female power as inherently good, constructive, noncompetitive, nurturing. I think of Audre Lorde's work, particularly the poem "Power," as an unusually courageous, head-on confrontation with this issue, remarkable in its refusal of easy, unconvincing resolutions.

Finally, I am struck by our determined repression of the magnitude of the destruction which stares us in the face: not just piecemeal, sniping attrition or agonizingly slow starvation—these have been commonplace throughout what we know of history—but the "*No* of no degrees,"[44] the definitive end of the human experiment. Nuclear war threatens to obliterate all of us. So does the only slightly more nebulous spectre of irreversible ecological imbalance. Yet feminist poetry (and theory) usually mention these terrors only obliquely, or as some kind of metaphor for generalized patriarchal destructiveness. (Chrystos' wrenchingly moving "No

Rock Scorns Me as Whore" in *This Bridge Called My Back* is an important recent exception.) Increasingly, I find myself turning to the work of Eastern European writers for their serious attempts to understand the nature of a machinery which is capable of this level of destruction.

Privilege, power, destruction: insofar as these are areas of tension, uneasiness, repression, they are also—as Rich's comment on Dickinson seems to suggest—extremely important areas for poetic exploration, if we are prepared to undergo the risk that exploration entails. Recently women of color have frequently taken the lead in these areas, perhaps because they have had far less opportunity to indulge in illusions of safety. But the challenge is there for all of us.

When I was on the verge of coming out, I remember picturing the lesbian-feminist community as a narrow, cloistered preserve separated from me by a high wall over which I would have to leap—a society both attractive and frightening in its purity. I imagined, I suppose, that the choice to undertake that leap would define, and simplify, the remainder of my life. Not to mention my poetry.

But there are no guarantees. Seven years later, I find myself very much alive in the world, confronted by all its choices and perplexities—companioned, yes; but equally alone. Aware that in creating a feminist context for women's poetry, we have created possibilities only, not certainties.

And convinced that the risk of poetry, the mingled danger and promise, are inseparable from the risk of life itself. Or, as Audre Lorde has written:

> And when the sun rises we are afraid
> it might not remain
> when the sun sets we are afraid
> it might not rise in the morning
> when our stomachs are full we are afraid
> of indigestion
> when our stomachs are empty we are afraid
> we may never eat again
> when we are loved we are afraid
> love will vanish

when we are alone we are afraid
love will never return
and when we speak we are afraid
our words will not be heard
nor welcomed
but when we are silent
we are still afraid .

So it is better to speak
remembering
we were never meant to survive.[45]

NOTES

[1] See, for example, Lorraine Bethel's "What Chou Mean *We*, White Girl?," *Conditions:Five* (1979), pp. 86-92.

[2] Gloria T. Hull discusses the (hitherto undervalued) role of women poets in the Harlem Renaissance in her "Afro-American Women Poets: A Bio-Critical Survey," *Shakespeare's Sisters: Feminist Essays on Women Poets*, eds. Sandra M. Gilbert and Susan Gubar (Bloomington: Indiana University Press, 1979), pp. 165-182.

[3] For an interesting discussion of the politics of genre as they affected nineteenth century British female novelists, see Gaye Tuchman and Nina Fortin, "Edging Women Out: Some Suggestions about the Structure of Opportunities and the Victorian Novel," *Signs*, Vol. 6, No. 2 (Winter, 1980), pp. 308-325.

[4] June Jordan's most recent poetry collection contains a fascinating and opinionated discussion of Whitman as the "father" of an anti-elitist "New World poetry." "For the Sake of a People's Poetry: Walt Whitman and the Rest of Us," *Passion* (Boston: Beacon Press, 1980), pp. ix-xxvi.

[5] Virginia Woolf, *A Room of One's Own* (New York: Harcourt, Brace, 1929, 1957), p. 70.

[6] Fran Winant, "Lesbians Publish Lesbians: My Life and Times with Violet Press," *Margins* No. 23 (August, 1975), p. 62.

[7] Adrienne Rich, "When We Dead Awaken: Writing as Re-Vision," *On Lies, Secrets, and Silence* (New York: Norton, 1979), pp. 48-49.

[8] "The only car I now own is a 1964 Rolls-Royce Silver Cloud....You can wear a skirt wherever you go and not suffer embarrassment when you step out of the Cloud...." (*Savvy*, April, 1981, p. 56). "I have my doubts about the Industrial Age and about the future of cars but never about my Rolls....Like any work of art, she is proof that humankind, in the midst of chaos, war and personal catastrophe, can still create something of enduring beauty" (p. 57).

[9] Elly Bulkin's "Introduction" to *Lesbian Poetry: An Anthology* (Persephone Press, 1981, pp. xxi-xxxiv) gives a good picture of the early "underground" feminist poets as outsiders in multiple senses.

[10] See Elly Bulkin for a discussion of the emergence of lesbian poetry. Also interesting in terms of this historical shift and the consciousness surrounding it is Adrienne Rich's discussion in *On Lies, Secrets, and Silence* of the controversy aroused by remarks she originally read at the Modern Language Association in December, 1976, published here as "It Is the Lesbian in Us..." (pp.199-202). I was present at that event

and vividly recall the alarm evinced by several feminist poets at her suggestion that "It is the lesbian in us who is creative" (p. 201).

[11]"When We Dead Awaken: Writing as Re-Vision," p. 49.

[12]"When We Dead Awaken: Writing as Re-Vision," p. 35.

[13]See Elly Bulkin, pp. xxvi-xxvii: "[Lesbian poets] sought to create a tradition that was...anti-hierarchical....The work of these early lesbian writers seems to be deliberately, perhaps even defiantly, 'anti-poetic'." For an extreme statement of an anti-patriarchal aesthetic, see Adrienne Parks, "The Lesbian Feminist as Writer as Lesbian Feminist," *Margins* No. 23 (August, 1975), p. 69.

[14]Karen Brodine, "Politics of Women Writing," *The Second Wave*, Vol. 5, No. 3 (1979), p. 9. See subsequent issues for correspondence discussing the ideas expressed in this article.

[15]Judy Grahn, "Murdering the King's English," *True to Life Adventure Stories*, Vol. I (Oakland: Diana Press, 1978), pp. 12-13.

[16]For revealing discussions of the experiences of creative writers within several revolutionary/Communist movements, I have found the following books particularly valuable: Daniel Aaron, *Writers on the Left* (New York: Avon Books, 1969); Czeslaw Milosz, *The Captive Mind* (New York: Vintage Books Edition, 1981); Jonathan D. Spence, *The Gate of Heavenly Peace: The Chinese and Their Revolution, 1895-1980* (New York: The Viking Press, 1981). The last volume contains extensive material on feminist/Communist writer of fiction Ding Ling. Notable for its sensitive treatment of both positive influences and negative constraints on a young American Communist writer is Deborah Rosenfelt's "From the Thirties: Tillie Olsen and the Radical Tradition," *Feminist Studies*, Vol. 7, No. 3 (1981), pp. 371-406.

[17]Olga Broumas, "Artemis," *Beginning with O* (New Haven: Yale University Press, 1977), p. 24.

[18]Adrienne Rich, "Cartographies of Silence," *The Dream of a Common Language* (New York: Norton, 1978), pp. 19-20.

[19]Adrienne Rich, "Power and Danger: Works of a Common Woman," *On Lies, Secrets, and Silence*, p. 247.

[20]Judith McDaniel, remarks transcribed in "The Transformation of Silence into Language and Action," *Sinister Wisdom* No. 6 (1978), p. 17.

[21]See, for example, Daly's remarks in "The Transformation of Silence into Language and Action," pp. 5-11 and *Gyn/Ecology: The Metaethics of Radical Feminism* (Boston: Beacon Press, 1978). See also Julia Penelope Stanley's remarks as the chair of that panel, and Marilyn Frye's "To Be and Be Seen: Metaphysical Misogyny," *Sinister Wisdom* No. 17 (1981), pp. 57-70.

[22]Negativity and pessimism have been charges frequently levelled

against male poets by feminists. "To the eye of a feminist, the work of Western male poets now writing reveals a deep, fatalistic pessimism as to the possibilities of change....," "When We Dead Awaken: Writing as Re-Vision," p. 49. For an interesting parallel, compare Czeslaw Milosz, p. 127: "[Polish Communist] critics upbraided him for his chief sins. They proclaimed that his work resembled depraved, or American, literature; that it was pessimistic; and that it lacked the element of 'conscious struggle,' i.e. struggle in the name of Communism." Milosz comments further on, "To approve convincingly is difficult, not because 'positive' values are incompatible with the nature of literature, but because approbation, in order to be effective, must be based on truth. The split between words and reality takes its revenge, even though the author be of good faith" (p. 237).

[23] The three quotations are from, respectively: Judy Grahn, "A Woman Is Talking to Death," *The Work of a Common Woman* (New York: St. Martin's Press, 1978), p. 131; June Jordan, "Poem About My Rights," *Passion*, p. 88; Susan Sherman, "Amerika," *Lesbian Poetry: An Anthology*, p. 59.

[24] Audre Lorde, "Poems Are Not Luxuries," *Chrysalis* No. 3 (1977), pp. 7-8.

[25] Osip Mandelstam, "Fourth Prose," *The Complete Critical Prose and Letters*, trans. Jane Gary Harris and Constance Link (Ann Arbor: Ardis, 1979), p. 324.

[26] Adrienne Parks, p. 69.

[27] In *Civil Wars*, (Boston: Beacon Press, 1981), pp. 59-73. See also "The Voice of the Children" in the same volume; Hope Landrine's "Culture, Feminist Racism & Feminist Classism: Blaming the Victim," *off our backs* (November, 1979), p. 2; and the numerous discussions of class, race, and language in *This Bridge Called My Back: Writings by Radical Women of Color*, eds. Cherríe Moraga and Gloria Anzaldúa (Persephone Press, 1981).

[28] Interview by Evelynn Hammonds, "Michelle Cliff Finds Her Own Voice," *Sojourner* (June, 1981), pp. 6 and 28.

[29] See Elly Bulkin's "Introduction" to *Lesbian Fiction: An Anthology* (Persephone Press, 1981) for a discussion of feminist perceptions of the possibilities for directly expressing personal experience in poetry, and the ways in which this may have influenced writers' choice of genre.

[30] June Jordan, "Thinking About My Poetry," *Civil Wars*, pp. 125-126.

[31] Melanie Kaye, "On Being a Lesbian-Feminist Artist," *We Speak in Code* (Pittsburgh: Motheroot Publications, 1980). Passages quoted are from pages 7, 8, and 9, respectively.

[32]Adrienne Rich, "Transcendental Etude," *The Dream of a Common Language*, p. 77.

[33]Adrienne Rich, "Power," *The Dream of a Common Language,* p. 3.

[34]Interview by Libby Woodwoman, "Pat Parker Talks about Her Life and Her Work," *Margins* No. 23, p. 61.

[35]See Becky Birtha's "Toward a Truly Feminist Criticism," *Sojourner*, Vol. 6, No. 2 (October, 1980), p. 4, for a practicing feminist critic's discussion of the destructive influence of traditional criticism upon attempts to develop feminist criticism.

[36]Marge Piercy, letter printed in "Responses" section, *Sinister Wisdom* No. 17 (1981), p. 105. For one example of forthright feminist criticism and the ensuing controversy, see Elly Bulkin, "Racism and Writing: Some Implications for White Lesbian Critics," *Sinister Wisdom* No. 13 (1980), pp. 3-22; and subsequent issues.

[37]June Jordan, "For the Sake of a People's Poetry: Walt Whitman and the Rest of Us."

[38]Reprinted in *Civil Wars*.

[39]"Pat Parker Talks about Her Life and Her Work," p. 61.

[40]Melanie Kaye, "On Being a Lesbian-Feminist Artist," p. 10.

[41]Feminist periodicals, traditionally the mainstay of feminist poetry publication, have also begun to exhibit a disdain for poetry in some cases. *Quest* recently announced its decision to cease publication of any poetry. The editors of the new quarterly *Common Lives/Lesbian Lives*, after soliciting submissions in sixteen categories of verbal and graphic forms not including poetry, and encouraging women to develop new forms, state, "Although CL/LL will be publishing poetry, the emphasis of the magazine will be on prose forms."

[42]Adrienne Rich, "Vesuvius at Home: The Power of Emily Dickinson," *On Lies, Secrets, and Silence*, pp. 174-175.

[43]Czeslaw Milosz, pp. 14-15.

[44]Adrienne Rich, "Phantasia for Elvira Shatayev," *The Dream of a Common Language*, p. 4.

[45]Audre Lorde, "A Litany for Survival," *The Black Unicorn* (New York: Norton, 1978), pp. 31-32.

Books by Jan Clausen:

After Touch (poems; Out & Out Books, 1975)

Waking at the Bottom of the Dark (poems; Long Haul Press, 1979). Order from Long Haul Press, P.O. Box 592, Van Brunt Station, Brooklyn, NY 11215. $3.00 + $.80 postage/handling.

Mother, Sister, Daughter, Lover (short stories; The Crossing Press, 1980). Order from The Crossing Press, Trumansburg, NY 14886. $4.95 + $.75 postage/handling.

To order additional copies of *A Movement of Poets*, send $.80 postage/handling per copy over cover price to Long Haul Press.